# AQA Science

Exclusively endorsed and approved by AQA

# Revision Guide

**Gerry Blake • Jo Locke**
Series Editor: Lawrie Ryan

## GCSE Additional Applied Science

Nelson Thornes
a Wolters Kluwer business

Text © Gerry Blake, Jo Locke 2006

Original illustrations © Nelson Thornes Ltd 2006

The right of Gerry Blake and Jo Locke to be identified as author of this work has been asserted by him/her in accordance with the Copyright, Designs and Patents Act 1988.

All rights reserved. No part of this publication may be reproduced or transmitted in any form or by any means, electronic or mechanical, including photocopy, recording or any information storage and retrieval system, without permission in writing from the publisher or under licence from the Copyright Licensing Agency Limited, of Saffron House, 6 - 10 Kirby Street, London EC1N 8TS.

Any person who commits any unauthorised act in relation to this publication may be liable to criminal prosecution and civil claims for damages.

Published in 2006 by:
Nelson Thornes Ltd
Delta Place
27 Bath Road
CHELTENHAM
GL53 7TH
United Kingdom

06 07 08 09 10 / 10 9 8 7 6 5 4 3 2 1

A catalogue record for this book is available from the British Library

ISBN-10: 0 7487 8321 0

ISBN-13: 978 0 7487 8321 2

Cover photographs: wheat field by Corel 555 (NT); fingerprints by Corel 565 (NT); snowboarder by Digital Vision XA (NT).

Cover bubble illustration by Andy Parker

Illustrations by Oxford Designers and Illustrators, Peters and Zabransky, and Roger Penwill

Page make-up by Design Practitioners Ltd

Printed and bound in Croatia by Zrinski

**Acknowledgements**

Alamy/Chris George 32, /David Reed 33, 36tl, /Foodfolio 2d, /Holt Studios International Ltd 2e, /Royalty Free 2b, BHSI 34tr, Empics 36c, Science Photo Library 15, /Gusto 2a, 15, /Alfred Pasieka17c(all), /Andrew Lambert 21l, cl, r, br (both), 24 /Andrew McClenaghan 11cl, Biophoto Associates 38l, /BSIP Roux 2c, BSIP Chassenet 36b, /David Scharf 7, /David Taylor 21cr, 25, /Dr Gary Gaugler 9, /Dr Jurgen Scriba 21bl, 23, /Eye of Science 18, /George Lepp, Agstock 9b, /James Holmes, Thomson Laboratories 20, /James King-Holmes 17cr, /Laguna Design 19, /Mauro Fermariello 17b, /Michael Donne 17tl, 38r /Nigel Cattlin, Holt Studios International Ltd 9t, /Phillipe Psaila 11b, 34, /Professor P M Motta, G Macchiarelli, S Anottola 4, /Samuel Ashfield 29, /Sususumu Nishinaga 39, /Tek Image 22t, /Topfoto 22b.

Every effort has been made to trace all the copyright holders, but if any have been overlooked the publisher will be pleased to make the necessary arrangements at the first opportunity.

With thanks to Stewart Chenery.

# How to revise

In Additional Applied Science, your Unit 1 and Unit 3 coursework portfolio carries 60% of your GCSE marks. We hope you followed the advice given in the Student Book and completed this to the best of your ability.

Unit 2 carries 40% of the marks and is assessed by a 1-hour written examination paper.

Unit 2 is based on three topics:
- Food science (Chapter 3)
- Forensic science (Chapter 4)
- Sports science (Chapter 5)

## Kinaesthetic (doing)
- Make revision cards.
- Highlight key words.
- Plan ahead – make a revision timetable.
- Seek advice from teachers / friends.
- Make quizzes for classmates. Swap!

## Visual (looking / drawing)
- Draw 'mind-maps'. Link together key ideas.
- Make big posters – especially of diagrams you might be asked to label.
- Use Post-it notes. Cover your bedroom furniture with key facts!
- Draw diagrams.

## Auditory (speaking / listening)
- Discuss ideas with others.
- Say ideas out loud.
- Ask your teachers questions.
- Get family and friends to test you regularly.

## How to Revise

## Practise questions
- Attempt the **Pre Tests** before you start revising each chapter. These help you to find out how much you already know, and what you need to do some more work on.
- Answer the **Check yourself** questions as you revise to see how much you are learning.
- Answer the **Exam-style questions** to find out what will be expected in the exam itself.
- Check the **Examples of exam answers** to see where marks could be gained.
- Answer the **Final exam paper**.

See page 42 for answers.

# Numeracy skills

On the foundation paper you will need to:
- Substitute numbers into a formula.
- Add, subtract, multiply and divide whole numbers and decimals.
- Use fractions, percentages and means (or averages).
- Understand differences in rates (i.e. how something changes per second).
- Use scales, tables and charts.
- Draw and interpret graphs.

On the higher paper you will also need to:
- Rearrange an equation.
- Convert between fractions, percentages and decimals.
- Use squares and square roots.
- Interpret graphs based on their gradient and on whether a relationship is directly or inversely proportional.

## Calculations

- When you need to calculate answers, don't forget to:
  - Remember your calculator!
  - Set your workings out carefully.
- In food science, you may need to analyse the contents of food and contrast organic and intensive farming.
- In forensic science, you may need to write the formula for an ionic compound and calculate the refractive index (= $\sin i / \sin r$).
- In sports science, you may need to calculate heart rate and breathing rate, basic daily energy requirements (BER = 1.3 kcal / hour / kg of body mass) and body mass index (BMI = mass / height$^2$ in units kg/m$^2$).

**Example 1**
Suppose you weigh 50 kg, what is your basic daily energy requirement?

Your BER = 1.3 kcal / hour / kg
= 1.3 × 50 kcal / hour
= 1.3 × 50 × 24 kcal / day
= 1560 kcal / day

**Example 2**
Suppose you weigh 50 kg and are 1.6 m tall, what is your body mass index?

Your BMI = $\frac{mass}{height^2}$

= $\frac{50 \, kg}{1.6^2 \, m^2}$

= 19.5 kg/m$^2$

- To work out an average, you add the numbers and divide by how many there are – just remember to press the = button before the dividing.
- Remember the rule for percentages: percentage = $\frac{is}{of} \times 100$

## Graphs

You need to be able to put information into, as well as take information off, tables, graphs and charts.

Whenever you see a table, graph or chart, *read it first* to see what it is about before reading the question.

**Remember the steps:**
- Label axes with name and unit. Choose a sensible scale (not in 3s).
- Plot points (small crosses in pencil).
- Draw (in pencil) a line of best fit (not zig-zags or snakes).

**Interpreting graphs:**
- Show (in pencil) corresponding values. 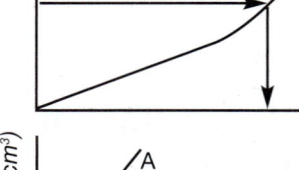
- Rate example: Rate of production is greater in A than B. 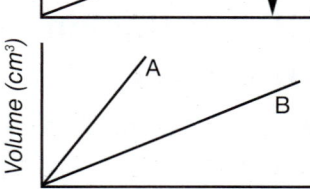
- (*Higher*) Gradient = $\frac{up}{across}$ = $\frac{y}{x}$ 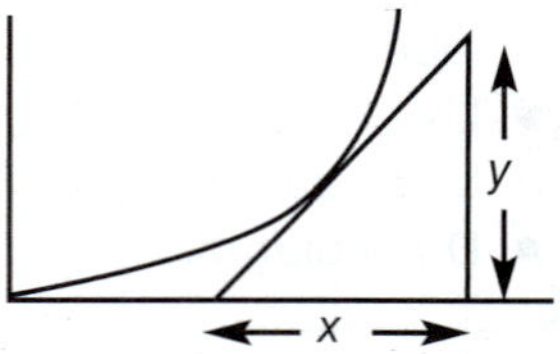
- (*Higher*)

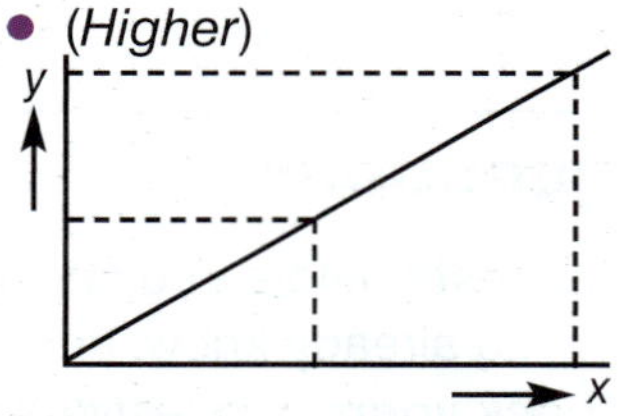

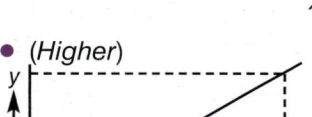

Directly proportional (double *x*: double *y*)

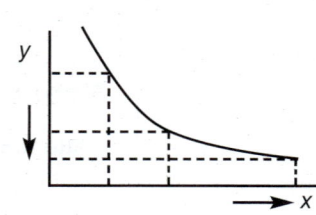

Inversely proportional (double *x*: halve *y*)

# Chapter 3 — Checklist: Food science

Tick when you have:
reviewed it after your lesson ✓ ☐ ☐
revised once – some questions right ✓ ✓ ☐
revised twice – all questions right ✓ ✓ ✓
Move on to another topic when you have all three ticks.

| | | |
|---|---|---|
| 3.1 Introduction to food science | 3.9 Using microorganisms in food production | |
| 3.2 Nutrients | 3.10 Food poisoning | |
| 3.3 Vitamins and minerals | 3.11 Growing crops | |
| 3.4 Vitamin deficiencies | 3.12 Rearing animals | |
| 3.5 How does your diet affect your health? (1) | 3.15 Testing food supplements for iron content | |
| 3.6 How does your diet affect your health? (2) | 3.16 The analysis of a fruit drink | |
| 3.7 What is in your food? | 3.18 Investigating bacterial growth | |
| 3.8 How can you tell what is in the food you are eating? | 3.19 Investigating the effects of nutrients on plant growth | |

# Chapter 3 — Pre Test: Food science

1. Name three uses of fat in the body.
2. What is the difference between a vitamin and a mineral?
3. What do we mean by the term 'RDA'?
4. What three factors affect your daily energy needs?
5. What problems does excess sodium cause in the body?
6. What are food additives?
7. How can you tell what the main ingredient is in a food product?
8. What is the word equation for fermentation?
9. What causes food poisoning?
10. Name four chemicals commonly used by intensive farmers.
11. Name two advantages of producing eggs by battery farming.

**students' book page 28**

## 3.1 Introduction to food science

### KEY POINTS

1. To remain healthy you must eat a balanced, healthy diet.
2. Food scientists and dieticians work in the Food Standards Agency to promote good eating habits, and to ensure that our food is safe and correctly labelled.
3. Some microorganisms in food products can cause food poisoning, but others are used to make useful products such as wine and cheese.
4. There are two main methods of farming – intensive and organic.

### CHECK YOURSELF

1. Name three useful products made using microorganisms.
2. What type of professional should an obese person seek advice from, to make changes to their diet to help them to lose weight?
3. Name some disadvantages of producing food intensively.

A healthy diet contains lots of fruit and vegetables. Most of your energy should be obtained from starchy foods such as pasta and rice and you should have a low intake of fat (especially saturated fat), salt and sugar. Eating a range of foods in the correct quantities is known as a balanced diet.

Dieticians study an individual's diet and advise on appropriate changes the person should make to eat a more healthy, balanced diet. They also prepare special diets for people who suffer with allergies or have food-related medical conditions such as diabetes.

Food scientists check that a food contains the same ingredients as those listed on the manufacturer's label. They use chemical tests to detect the presence of nutrients in foods, chemical additives and microorganisms.

Harmful microorganisms present in food can cause food poisoning, so strict hygiene and cleaning procedures must be followed to prevent food contamination. Once prepared, food must be stored properly to prevent it 'going off'. However, some microorganisms are used to produce useful food and drink products. For example bacteria are used in cheese and yoghurt production, and yeast is used to make beer, bread and wine.

Most of the world's food is produced intensively. This technique involves the use of chemicals to protect plants and animals from disease, competition, being eaten and to enhance growth. These chemicals maximise yields. However, they can enter food chains killing untargeted animals. The use of large machinery can also damage the environment.

Organic farmers do not use artificial chemicals. This results in a more natural product, and provides better living conditions for animals. However, yields are generally much smaller. This results in more expensive products than those produced by more intensive means.

**students' book page 30**

## 3.2 Nutrients

### KEY POINTS

1. Nutrients are essential elements or compounds that your body needs to carry out the vital life functions of respiration, movement, growth and repair of body tissue.
2. You need to know the function of carbohydrates, saturated and unsaturated fats, fibre, vitamins and minerals, and proteins.

### EXAM HINTS

**Be careful with time!**
If you get stuck on a question, miss it out. Don't spend time worrying about it. You may have time to come back to it later.

| Food group | Role in the body | Examples of food |
|---|---|---|
| **Carbohydrates:** | | |
| **Simple** (sugars) | Main source of energy | |
| **Complex** (starches) | Have to be broken down by the body into simple sugars | |
| **Proteins** | Needed for repairing body tissues, growth and energy. Your body uses the protein you eat to make specialised protein molecules; for example, haemoglobin. | |
| **Fats – saturated and unsaturated** | Store of energy, keep you warm, cover your vital organs, protecting them from damage and provide a source of fat-soluble vitamins | |
| **Vitamins and minerals** | Needed in small quantities to keep you healthy | |
| **Fibre** | Form of carbohydrate that is not digested, but adds bulk to your food so that waste can be pushed out of the digestive system more easily. Fibre also absorbs poisonous waste made when we digest food. | |

**BUMP UP YOUR GRADE**
Make sure you know what the key words mean.

**CHECK YOURSELF**
1 What is protein used for in the body?
2 Why must you eat fibre even though it provides you with no nutrients?

students' book page 32

## 3.3 Vitamins and minerals

**KEY POINT**
Vitamins and minerals are needed by your body in small amounts so that it can grow, develop and function normally.

Vitamins are chemical compounds. They perform many functions in the human body:
- Vitamin A (found in carrots, for example) helps to maintain healthy eyesight and skin, and keeps mucous membranes (like the nose and mouth) free from infection.
- Vitamin B vitamins (a group of vitamins) are involved in releasing energy from carbohydrate foods and nerve functions. Nuts are a good source of vitamin B.
- Vitamin C (found in fruits) maintains your immune system, helps absorb iron and maintains your skin and linings of the digestive system.
- Vitamin D (found in fatty fish) helps absorb calcium and phosphorus and is needed to form healthy teeth and bones.
- Vitamin K (found in dark green vegetables) aids blood clotting.
- **Fat-soluble vitamins** (A, D, E and K) are stored in your fatty tissues and the liver until you need them.
- **Water-soluble vitamins** (B and C) must be used by your body straight away, otherwise they pass out of your body in urine.

Minerals are chemical elements needed by your body. They include:
- Iron (found in spinach and liver), which helps your body to manufacture haemoglobin.
- Phosphorus (found in fish and eggs), which is involved in releasing energy from your food.
- Calcium (found in dairy products), which is important for healthy teeth and bones.
- Zinc (found in meat and seafood) plays an important role in healing wounds and enzyme action.

**Key words: vitamins, minerals**

**GET IT RIGHT!**
If a question asks you for one thing only, do *not* give more than one answer. If you write a correct answer, and then a wrong answer as well, you will lose the mark you should have been given.

**CHECK YOURSELF**
1 Name two examples of vitamins and two examples of minerals.
2 What is the role of iron in the body?
3 Name three sources of vitamin K.

students' book page 34

## 3.4 Vitamin deficiencies

### KEY POINTS

1. If you do not take in the **Recommended Daily Allowance (RDA)** of a vitamin through food or drink you are said to have a vitamin deficiency.
2. Vitamin deficiencies can cause unpleasant symptoms and diseases.

**Key words: vitamin deficiency**

### EXAM HINTS

**Read the question carefully!**
If the question asks you to 'describe' – write what happens (for a process, such as brewing beer), or list the features (for example, of a person suffering a vitamin deficiency).

| Vitamin deficiency | Symptoms | Possible solutions |
|---|---|---|
| A | Dry skin and mucous membranes – these line your throat, nose, mouth and lungs. Difficulties in your eyes adjusting to dim light – 'night blindness'. | Eat raw carrots |
| B | Mouth sores and the degeneration of nerves. Anaemia – not enough red blood cells are made; this means that your blood cannot carry enough oxygen, resulting in you feeling very tired and dizzy. | Eat a handful of nuts |
| C | Soft and bleeding gums, slow-healing wounds, bruising and nosebleeds – without vitamin C the walls of your blood vessels are weak and can rupture easily allowing blood to escape. Severe deficiency can lead to the disease scurvy. | Eat plenty of fresh fruit and vegetables |
| D | Weak teeth and bones – vitamin D helps bones absorb calcium, without which they are soft and flexible. Severe deficiency can lead to the disease rickets. | Eat cereals – many are fortified with vitamin D |

### CHECK YOURSELF

1. If you suffered from the disease scurvy, what vitamin is your body lacking?
2. What are the symptoms of vitamin A deficiency?

students' book page 36

## 3.5 How does your diet affect your health? (1)

### KEY POINT

1. Eaten in large quantities, sugar, salt, fat (especially saturated fat) and food additives can have a significant effect on your health now and, more severely, later in life.

Food provides your body with the energy it needs to function properly. The amount of energy (measured in kilojoules, kJ) you need depends on your age, your body size and how active you are. You need energy even if you are not 'doing' anything – to power your organs, maintain your body temperature and keep all the chemical reactions in your body going.

Saturated fat, contained in animal products like butter and cheese, can increase your blood cholesterol levels. Excess cholesterol sticks to the walls of your arteries. This causes them to narrow, slowing blood flow. The walls of the artery become rough, which can cause the blood to clot, blocking the vessel.

Partially blocked arteries can cause chest pains (**angina**). Total blockage can cause a heart attack, because the oxygen supply is cut off completely.

**Key words: saturated fats**

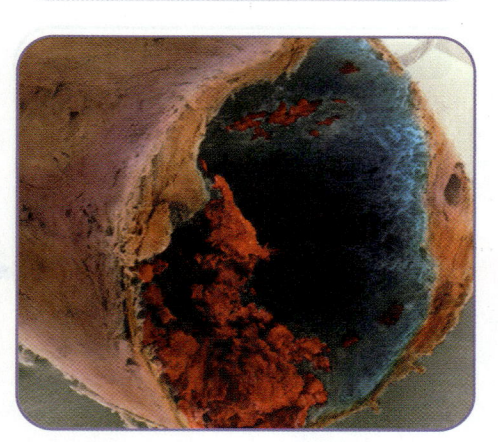

This photograph shows a blood clot (red) in a coronary artery

### EXAM HINTS

**Check your answers!**
When you have finished your exam, try to leave enough time to go back over your answers. You can often pick up lots of extra marks this way.

### CHECK YOURSELF

1. Name some foods that contain saturated fat.
2. What happens if you have too much cholesterol in your body?

## 3.6 How does your diet affect your health? (2)

*students' book page 38*

### KEY POINTS

1. Excess sugar in your diet can lead to weight gain and, eventually, obesity. This increases your risk of developing diabetes.
2. Excess sodium (salt) in your diet increases blood pressure, which over time can result in heart disease, kidney damage and strokes.

Sugar is a simple carbohydrate used to sweeten food and improve texture. Sugars provide instant energy, as they are absorbed quickly, but have little nutritional value. Eating too much sugar can lead to weight gain and eventually **obesity**.

Obese people significantly increase their likelihood of developing type 2 diabetes. In this condition a person's blood sugar level is too high as the body is not producing enough insulin, or the cells do not use insulin properly. Insulin is a hormone that regulates blood sugar levels by removing excess sugar from the blood. Diabetes can lead to serious complications such as heart disease, strokes and blindness.

Sodium (in the form of common salt) is needed by the body to regulate blood pressure and blood volume. It is also critical for the functioning of muscles and nerves. Sodium occurs naturally in most foods, and is even found in drinking water. Excess intake of sodium can cause **high blood pressure**. Over time this can damage your arteries, putting a strain on your heart. In general, the higher your blood pressure, the greater your risk of developing heart disease, kidney damage and having a stroke.

**Key words:** sugars, diabetes, sodium chloride (salt), insulin

### CHECK YOURSELF

1. Why does your body need sodium?
2. What role does insulin play in the body?

## 3.7 What is in your food?

*students' book page 40*

### KEY POINTS

1. There are three main reasons why manufacturers add chemicals (additives) to foods:
   - To keep food fresh for longer periods of time.
   - To replace / enhance the flavour of food that may be lost when the food is processed.
   - To improve the appearance of foods.
2. There are advantages and disadvantages in using food additives.

| Additive | Use | Example | Found in foods such as: |
|---|---|---|---|
| Antioxidants | Reduce the chance of fats and oils oxidising. This causes food to change colour or go rancid. | Vitamin C (ascorbic acid) | Meat products, mayonnaise, bakery products and sauces |
| Flavourings Flavour enhancers | Add a particular taste or smell to a food. Bring out the flavour in food without adding a flavour of their own. | Monosodium glutamate. MSG-sensitive individuals can experience nausea, headaches and breathing difficulties. | Processed foods like pre-prepared meals, soups, and sausages |
| Food colourings | Improve the appearance of foods. | Curcumin – natural yellow extract of turmeric roots. Tartrazine (E102) – artificial colouring (linked with child hyperactivity). | Cakes, curry |
| Preservatives | Help to keep food safe for longer – to preserve some foods. | Sugar, salt and vinegar are still used. The toxic nature of some preservatives, e.g. benzoic acid, may be harmful. | Jam, fruit juices, yoghurts and soft drinks |
| Sweeteners | Sweeten food. They contain very little energy and are better for your teeth than sugar. | Aspartame and saccharin – both have been linked with cancer in laboratory tests. | Diet drinks |
| Thickeners (emulsifiers, stabilisers, gelling agents) | Help mix together ingredients that would normally separate. Thicken food. | Starch | Gravy |

**Key words:** food additive, antioxidant, flavour enhancer, food colouring, preservatives, sweeteners, thickeners

### CHECK YOURSELF

1. What do preservatives do?
2. Give a disadvantage of using preservatives.
3. Why do many parents not allow their children to eat food that contains lots of colourings?

## 3.8 How can you tell what is in the food you are eating?

students' book page 42

### KEY POINT
Food labels provide information about the ingredients the food or drink contains, including any additives, advice on how you should store the product and the nutritional value it gives you.

### EXAM HINTS
**Make sure you use units!** Numerical questions require you to use units. There is often a mark available for writing the correct unit on an answer.

Food labels contain the following information:
- **Ingredients** – listed in descending order of weight (including chemical additives).
- **A 'best before' date** – this refers to the quality of a product. When the date runs out the food is not usually harmful, but may begin to lose its flavour and texture.
- **A 'use by' date** – this refers to the safety of the substance you are eating. Eating or drinking a product after this date puts your health at risk.
- **A 'sell by' or 'display until' date** – this is used by some shops to help with stock control.
- **Nutritional information** – how much energy, protein, fat, carbohydrate, fibre and sodium the food contains.
- Ingredients that people may be **allergic or intolerant** to, like nuts and gluten.
- **Storage conditions** – if followed incorrectly, the food may 'go off' quickly.

This is an example of a food label. Manufacturers are required by law to state what ingredients their product contains.

At the moment there is no law stating what 'low fat' means. There is often little difference between a 'low fat' biscuit and the manufacturer's standard version. To check for yourself you need to compare the nutritional information section on the label.

**'GM free'** products contain no genetically modified plants and animals – those that have had their genes altered by scientists to produce desirable features like frost and pest resistance, and higher yields.

**Key words: ingredients, genetically modified (GM)**

### CHECK YOURSELF
1. Name two ingredients that require labelling that people may be allergic or intolerant to.
2. What is the difference between a 'best before' and a 'use by' date?

## 3.9 Using microorganisms in food production

*students' book page 44*

### KEY POINTS

1. Bacteria and fungi play an important role in the production of many foods and drinks. Bacteria are used to ferment milk sugars in both cheese and yoghurt production.
2. Yeast (a fungus) is used to ferment maltose to make beer, grape sugars to make wine and sugar to make bread.

The ideal conditions for fermentation are a good supply of glucose, no oxygen present, and a temperature between 15°C and 25°C. Fermentation can be summarised by the equation:

$$\text{glucose} \rightarrow \text{ethanol} + \text{carbon dioxide}$$
$$C_6H_{12}O_6 \rightarrow 2C_2H_5OH + 2CO_2$$

**To make bread:**
- Flour, water, sugar and yeast are mixed to make dough. Enzymes in the yeast ferment the sugar into ethanol and carbon dioxide. As the gas is trapped inside the dough, it makes the dough rise.
- The dough is then baked. In the oven the ethanol evaporates. The bubbles of carbon dioxide gas expand, making the bread rise further.

**To make beer:**
- Malted barley grains (malt) are mixed with warm water, which converts the starch in the barley into maltose (sugar).
- Hops are added for flavour and the liquid is boiled.
- Once cooled, yeast is added to ferment maltose into alcohol – beer.

**To make wine:**
- Grapes are crushed.
- Yeast is added. Yeast changes the grape sugars into alcohol.

**To make cheese:**
- Bacteria are added to milk to convert lactose (milk sugar) into lactic acid.
- Rennet is also added as it contains rennin (an enzyme) that changes milk protein into casein (curd).
- The milk curdles and separates into curds and whey.
- Whey (mainly water) is drained off and the curds pressed and left to ripen to improve flavour and consistency.

**To make yoghurt:**
- Milk is boiled and bacteria are added.
- The milk is kept warm for several hours, allowing the bacteria to multiply and ferment lactose. The lactic acid produced curdles the milk into yoghurt and restrains the growth of harmful bacteria. 'Live' yoghurts have not been pasteurised to kill the bacteria used to make the yoghurt.

**Key words:** yeast, fermentation, bacteria, fungi

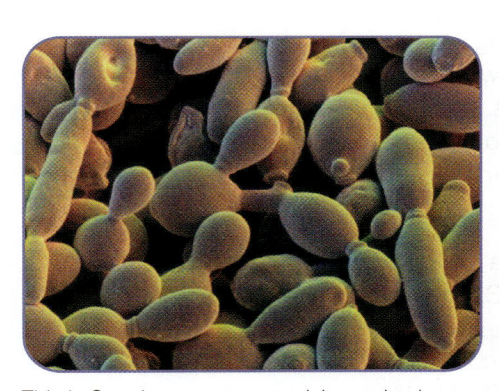

*This is Saccharomyces cerevisiae – also known as baker's or brewer's yeast*

### GET IT RIGHT!

**Read the question carefully.**
If the question asks you to *explain* a process – do not just describe it. You also need to say *why* things happen.

### EXAM HINTS

**Note how the examiner wants you to write an answer.**
If the question says 'Give the word equation for fermentation', write your answer in words – for example you need to write 'carbon dioxide' *not* 'CO₂'

### CHECK YOURSELF

1. Name two products that are produced by yeast fermenting sugar.
2. Why does bread not contain alcohol?

**students' book page 46**

## 3.10 Food poisoning

### KEY POINTS

1. Food poisoning is caused by the growth of microorganisms in food. The most serious types of food poisoning are due to bacteria and the toxins they produce.
2. Good hygiene practices reduce the risk of contamination. Proper storage and cooking can kill bacteria.

### CHECK YOURSELF

1. What are the common symptoms of food poisoning?
2. Between which temperatures do bacteria grow most rapidly?
3. How does pickling help to preserve foods?

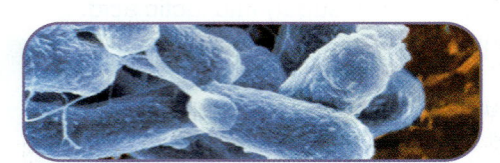

This is *E.coli 0157*. Bacteria multiply rapidly – in the right conditions one bacterium can multiply to more than 4 million in just 8 hours. To do so they need moisture, food, and warmth.

There are three main groups of bacteria that cause food poisoning:
- *Campylobacter* – found in raw meat, un-pasteurised milk, and untreated water. This is the most common cause of food poisoning.
- *Salmonella* – found in raw meat, eggs, unwashed vegetables and un-pasteurised milk.
- *E. coli* – there are many different types e.g. *E. coli 0157* can cause severe illness and is found in raw and undercooked meats, un-pasteurised milk and dairy products.

Common signs of food poisoning are stomach pains, diarrhoea, vomiting and fever. Most people get better within a few days, though in rare cases food poisoning can kill.

Microorganisms are very hard to detect, as they do not usually affect the taste, appearance or smell of food. To prevent food contamination, steps that should be followed include:
- Good personal hygiene practices, e.g. washing hands, covering cuts.
- Using detergents to ensure the working area remains clean.
- Using disinfectants to kill bacteria on work surfaces.
- The use of sterile packaging materials.
- Disposing of waste into appropriate containers.
- Adequate control of pests, e.g. flying insects, mice.

Bacteria can be killed by:
- **Changing the temperature** – bacteria multiply rapidly between 5°C and 65°C. Above 70°C most are killed. Below 5°C most multiply very slowly, if at all and at very low temperatures some will die. However, many begin to multiply again if conditions warm up.
- **Pickling** – acid is added, which kills most bacteria, e.g. pickled onions.
- **Salting** – bacteria become dehydrated and die, or temporarily inactivated e.g. bacon.
- **Drying** – bacteria need water for growth. Without water their growth will slow and eventually stop, e.g. rice.

**Key words: food poisoning, microorganisms, sterile**

---

**students' book page 48**

## 3.11 Growing crops

### KEY POINTS

1. There are two main types of farming – intensive and organic.
2. Intensive farming relies on the use of a range of chemicals to produce crops with high yields.
3. Organic farming generally produces fewer crops from the same area of land but no chemicals are used, so many people think the food tastes better and is healthier.

- **Intensive farming** produces large quantities of food cheaply and efficiently by maximising the growth of crops and farm animals. Controlled environments and a number of different chemicals are used to achieve this.
- **Organic farming** uses natural methods of producing crops and rearing animals. Artificial chemicals are not used and animals are allowed to roam as freely as possible. Many people believe food grown in this way is healthier and tastes better, and are willing to pay more for products produced like this.

Ladybirds are used by gardeners and farmers to eat aphids

## AQA EXAMINER SAYS...

**Intensive v. organic farming**
Questions on farming are very common in the Additional Applied Science exam. Make sure you know the main differences between the two types of farming.

## CHECK YOURSELF

1. How do organic farmers remove weeds from their fields?
2. How do organic farmers replace nutrients in the soil that are lost through crop harvesting?

To produce a high yield of crops, farmers need to control the following factors:

| Factor controlled | Intensive methods | Organic methods |
|---|---|---|
| **Nutrient content of soil** – for healthy growth, plants need nitrogen, phosphorus, potassium and magnesium. As crops grow, they remove these from the soil, so they need to be constantly replaced. | Adding chemical **fertilisers** – most commonly NPK fertiliser. | Adding manure or compost. Rotating crops, as different crops take different nutrients from the soil. Planting leguminous plants like clover, which add nitrates to the soil. |
| **Pests**, e.g. aphids, locusts and beetles. | Spraying crops with chemical **pesticides**, which kill the insects. | **Biological control** – predators (normally insects) are grown in large numbers, then released onto the crops where they eat the pests. Moulds and fungi can be used to kill the pests, by infecting the pests with a disease. Selective breeding of pests and disease-resistant crops. |
| **Weeds** – other plants that would compete with the crop for water, nutrients and space. | Spraying with chemical **herbicides**, which kill weeds. | Removing weeds by hand, or using machines. This method works well on crops that are grown in rows, such as vegetables. |
| **Fungi** | Spraying with chemical **fungicides**, which kill fungi. | Growing strong healthy crops to combat disease. Removing infected plant material and disposing of it, normally by burning. |

**Key words:** intensive farming, organic farming, fertiliser, pesticide, herbicide, fungicide, biological control

---

students' book page 50 — **3.12 Rearing animals**

## KEY POINTS

1. Intensively farmed animals are kept in a strictly controlled environment, which makes the animals increase in size quickly. This makes intensively farmed animals and their products cheaper.
2. Organically farmed animals are kept under more natural conditions.

Battery-farmed hens are kept in a carefully controlled environment, which significantly increases egg production but unfortunately reduces the hen's life expectancy.

Intensively-reared animals are kept in strictly-controlled environments. This makes the animals increase in size quickly, so the animals and their products become cheaper. However, some people are concerned about the animals' well-being and believe they are kept in unethical conditions.

These are the main differences between intensive and organic farming of animals:

| Factors that can be controlled | Intensively reared animals | Organically reared animals |
|---|---|---|
| Food supply | • Animals are fed a high-protein diet to rapidly increase their body mass. | • Organic food is fed to the animals. |
| Temperature | • Animals are kept indoors, in a warm environment. Animals waste less energy heating their own bodies. | • Animals normally live outdoors, but may be kept inside in harsh weather. |
| Space | • Restricted movement. Animals do not waste energy moving around. | • Animals are allowed to roam as freely as possible. |
| Use of drugs | • Growth hormones are often given to animals to speed up their growth.<br>• Antibiotics are often given to animals to prevent the spread of disease. | • Animals are not given artificial growth hormones.<br>• Antibiotics are not used unless an animal is ill. |
| Safety of enclosure | • Animals are kept safe from predators. | • Animals are often kept indoors at night to protect them from predators. |

### BUMP UP YOUR GRADE

If you are asked to compare the two types of farming, make sure that you stick to the facts. Answers such as 'Intensive farming is cruel' will not gain credit. To gain a mark you could say 'Some people think intensive farming is cruel, as animals are often kept in very small spaces'.

### CHECK YOURSELF

1. Name two situations in which organically reared animals are kept inside.
2. Why are intensively reared animals fed a high-protein diet?

This table is a comparison between battery-farmed and free-range egg production:

| Condition | Battery | Free-range |
|---|---|---|
| Egg production | • About 300 eggs a year | • About 30 eggs a year |
| Egg price | • Cheap | • Expensive |
| Minimum space allowed | • 550 $cm^2$ per bird | • An acre of field for every 400 chickens – over 1 million $cm^2$ per bird! |
| Access to outside | • None | • Free to roam during daylight hours, but shelter provided |
| Environment | • Light conditions can be altered to depict spring, with long daylight hours. This is when hens naturally lay more eggs, so this increases egg production. | • Outside – natural. Inside – space is provided for the hens to move around and perch. Specially developed nest boxes give the birds the quiet and security they need to lay. |
| Health problems caused by environment in which animals are kept | • Foot deformities caused by the absence of suitable perches and movement restrictions.<br>• Prone to multiple fractures, caused by bone weakness – high egg production results in calcium deficiency. | • None |

**Key words: intensive farming, organic farming**

---

## 3.15 Testing food supplements for iron content

*students' book page 60*

### KEY POINTS

1. People need to be aware of the precise amount of iron they take in a supplement. Too much can be toxic, and too little would not alleviate the symptoms from which they are suffering.
2. Scientists working in quality control regularly sample products to ensure that their contents exactly match the description of the product.

The iron content of a food supplement can be measured using the following procedure:

- Dissolve the tablets being tested in sulfuric acid ($H_2SO_4$).
- Titrate potassium manganate(VII) solution ($KMnO_4$) from a burette against the iron tablet solution.
- The iron tablet solution will change from colourless to pale pink at the end point of titration.
- Record the volume of potassium manganate(VII) used in the titration.
- Use a calibration graph (like the one below) to calculate the mass of iron in the tablets that were tested.

### CHECK YOURSELF

1. What colour is potassium manganate(VII) solution?
2. How do you know when the end point of this titration is reached?

### BUMP UP YOUR GRADE

Make sure you know the chemical formulae for common chemicals, e.g. sulfuric acid is $H_2SO_4$. You may be asked simply to write down the formula for a chemical, or to write out a full chemical equation in symbols.

The mass of iron tablets

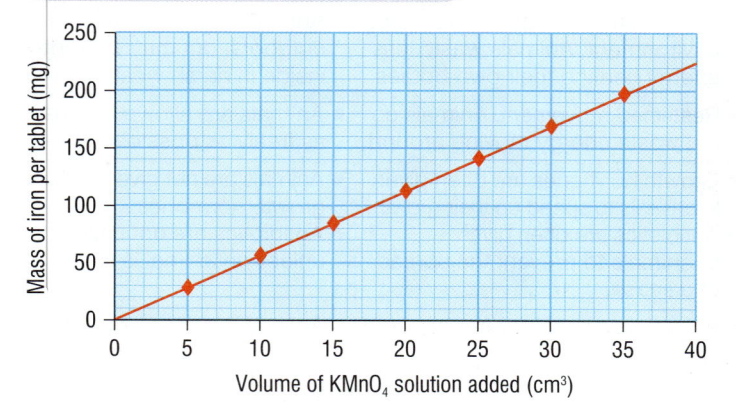

**Key words: iron content, titration**

**students' book page 62**

## 3.16 The analysis of a fruit drink

### KEY POINTS

1. Qualitative tests detect the presence of a substance.
2. Quantitative tests tell you how much of a substance is present.

Common qualitative tests performed by food scientists are listed in the table below:

| Substance testing for | Reagent | Colour change expected |
|---|---|---|
| starch | iodine | orange → blue-black |
| fat | ethanol | clear → cloudy |
| protein | Biuret | pale blue → purple |
| sugar: glucose | Benedict's solution | blue → orange / red |
| sucrose | Benedict's solution + hydrochloric acid | blue → orange / red |
| acidity | universal indicator solution | use the universal indicator colour scale to read pH |

Common quantitative tests performed by food scientists include:

- **Moisture content by evaporation** This measures how much liquid is in a food product.
  The mass of the food being tested is determined using a balance (mass 1). It is placed in an oven overnight at 40 °C, and the mass of the food is taken again (mass 2). The following calculation is then used:

$$\text{Moisture content (\% by mass)} = \frac{\text{mass 1} - \text{mass 2}}{\text{mass 1}} \times 100$$

- **Suspended matter by filtration** This tells you how much solid material is present in a liquid.
  The total mass of the liquid is determined before passing it through a dried filter paper. The filter paper and residue are then dried and the mass of the filtrate measured. The following calculation is then used:

$$\text{Suspended matter (\% by mass)} = \frac{\text{mass of residue}}{\text{original mass of liquid}} \times 100$$

- **Vitamin C content** This technique compares the vitamin C content of different foods.
  The food solution is placed in a burette. A fixed volume of DCPIP indicator (blue) is placed in a conical flask. Then the food sample is run into the indicator until the indicator is decolourised. The more food solution required to decolourise the indicator, the less vitamin C is in the food.
- **Acidity of a product by titration** This tests how acidic liquids are.
  A fixed volume of sodium hydroxide (NaOH) is added to a conical flask, with phenolphthalein indicator (pink). The food solution is placed in a burette, and titrated against the sodium hydroxide. The volume of food solution required to neutralise the alkali (when the indicator goes colourless) is found. To calculate the concentration of the food product an appropriate formula can then be used.

**Key words: qualitative, quantitative, food tests**

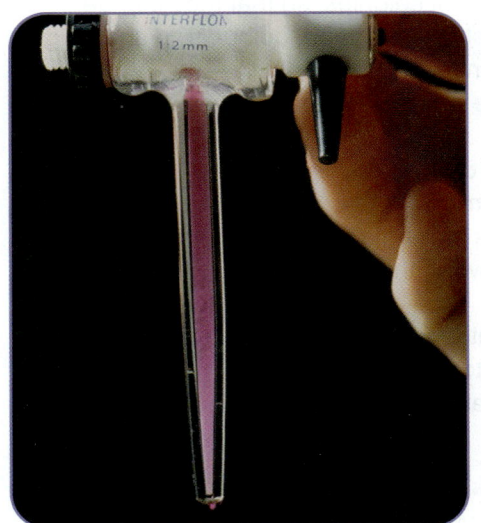

Burette

Pipette

### CHECK YOURSELF

1. What indicator is used to detect the presence of vitamin C?
2. What is the difference between a qualitative and quantitative food test?

### GET IT RIGHT!

Make sure you learn the table above which shows the colour changes which take place in the qualitative food tests. These are straightforward tests: if a colour change occurs when a reagent is added, then the food substance being tested for must be present.

## 3.17 Investigating bacterial growth

### KEY POINTS

1. Microbiologists use serial dilutions to count bacteria and produce streak plates to identify the species of bacteria they are studying.
2. All techniques are carried out under aseptic conditions to prevent unwanted microorganisms entering or passing from a sample to a microbiologist.

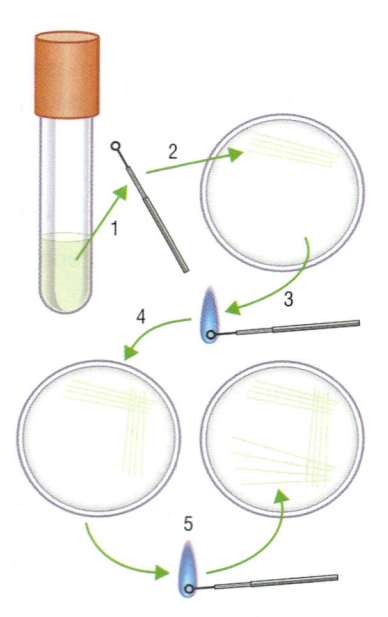

The following techniques are commonly used by microbiologists:

- **Aseptic technique**
  Microorganisms are often transferred from one area to another with a wire loop. To sterilise the loop, it is heated in a Bunsen burner flame until it glows red, then allowed to cool. Whilst cooling, the loop is held close to the flame away from the bench to ensure it remains sterile.
- **Sampling the environment**
  A sterile cotton swab is used to sample bacteria on a surface by rubbing the swab on the surface, then lightly on the surface of an agar plate. The agar plates are then incubated for about 48 hours to allow any microorganisms present to grow.
- **Making a streak plate**
  This technique isolates individual bacterial colonies, so that they can be identified. Colonies differ in characteristics like shape, colour, size and height.
  1. Dip a sterilised wire loop into the sample of bacteria.
  2. Make four or five streaks across one edge of an agar plate.
  3. Flame and cool the loop.
  4. Make a second series of streaks by crossing over the first set, picking up some of the cells and spreading them out across a new section of the plate.
  5. Repeat steps 3 and 4 two more times making a third and fourth set of streaks.
  6. Incubate the plate upside down allowing the cells to form colonies.
- **Serial dilutions**
  Diluting a bacterial sample spreads out the bacteria, so individual colonies of bacteria can be cultured when added to an agar plate.
  Number of bacteria (per $cm^3$) in original sample = number of colonies * dilution of the sample

**Key words: aseptic technique, streak plate, serial dilutions**

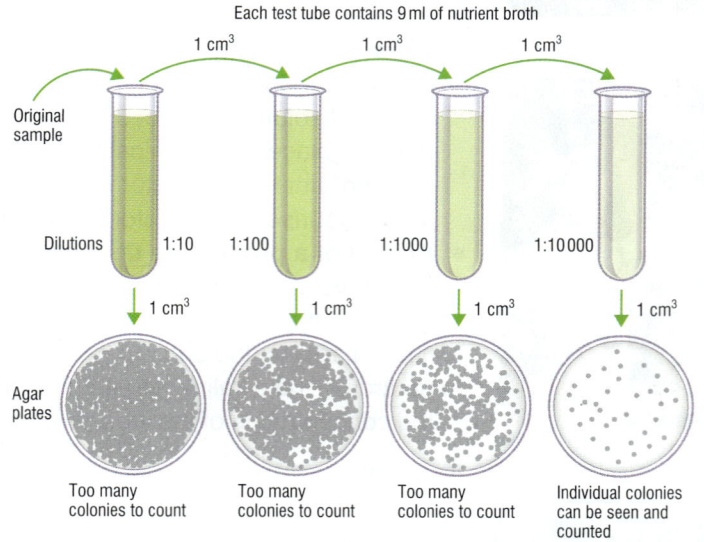

How to make a streak plate

Carrying out a serial dilution

### EXAM HINTS

**Practise using equations.**
Normally in an exam question you will be provided with an equation if you need to calculate something, e.g. the number of bacteria in the original sample. Practise reading questions and inserting the data you are given into a formula. Make sure you are confident at addition, subtraction, multiplication and division.

### CHECK YOURSELF

1. What technique would you use to count the number of bacteria in a sample?
2. Why should you always use aseptic technique when working with microorgansims?

*Private Schools Illustrated — 1158*

# THE GULLIVER SCHOOLS

Mrs. Marian Krutulis, *Director*
Mr. John Krutulis, *Associate Director*

Gulliver Schools offers an integrated and comprehensive college preparatory program from primary school through grade twelve. With five campuses located in Coral Gables, South Miami, Village of Pinecrest, and Miami Dade County, Gulliver Schools enjoys the quiet beauty of residential communities, while having access to the cultural amenities of the greater Miami area. Gulliver Schools is in close proximity to the University of Miami, Miami-Dade Community College, and Florida International University. The community offers a wealth of cultural opportunities, as well as a multilingual international population.

Gulliver is proud that its student body reflects the multiethnic and multiracial character of South Florida. In order to accommodate our growing international population, students are offered the opportunity to earn the International Baccalaureate diploma. This prestigious, internationally recognized program is designed as a comprehensive two-year curriculum. It commences in the junior year, and allows its graduates the opportunity to fulfill the requirements of university systems worldwide. Gulliver Preparatory is the only private school in South Florida offering this diploma.

Gulliver's traditional college preparatory curriculum centers on the essential core curriculum: English, social studies, science, mathematics, foreign language, and visual and performing arts. Enrichment is provided with elective and required courses in computer science, art history, humanities, philosophy, video technology production, journalism, the classics, and physical education. Classes are suited to the various levels of students' abilities and include advanced placement (21 courses offered), enriched, honors, and college preparatory courses.

For busy parents with tight work schedules, Hackley's five-day boarding program offers their child an attractive alternative to urban day school. Hackley provides a rigorous, traditional and personalized education to able and motivated students whose parents value education. In 2004, 158 students took 360 Advanced Placement exams. 94% of scores were a 3 or better. In 2004, there were 2 National Merit Scholars, 9 National Merit Semifinalists, and 21 Commended Students. In 2004, there were 2 winners of the prestigious Robert C. Byrd Honors Scholarship. In the last five years, 8 seniors were National Hispanic Scholars. The greatest number of recent graduates are now attending Boston University, Columbia, Cornell, George Washington University, Harvard, NYU, University of Pennsylvania, Princeton, and Yale.

Situated on a 285-acre campus on a hilltop overlooking the Hudson, Hackley is a day and 5-day boarding school. Hackley offers a full sports program, extracurricular and community service activities, and a rich range of visual arts and performing arts opportunities. A member of the New York City Independent School Ivy League, Hackley's 62 teams play schools, which are a subway ride from their parents' offices. Only twenty-four miles from Manhattan, the School's fields, tennis courts, and swimming pool are an easy drive or train ride for parents who want to attend Friday afternoon or weekend games and other events. A typical boarder's day could include five or six academic classes, music lessons in the Performing Arts Center, film developing in the photography lab, lacrosse practice, free time before dinner, and a structured, supervised study time in the evenings. Students have time to forge life-long friendships. The diversity of the student body allows them to enlarge and connect their worlds from the classroom, the playing field, and the boarding corridor to their homes in the tri-state area.

For further information, contact: Julie S. Core, Director of Admission, 914-366-2642.

*Private Schools Illustrated — 1162*

# HARGRAVE MILITARY ACADEMY
## CHATHAM, VA

Dr. Wheeler Baker,
Col., USMC (Retired), *President*

Since 1909, Hargrave Military Academy has been fulfilling its main objective—helping students to discover their capabilities. Located on nearly 200 acres, Hargrave is 18 miles north of Danville, Virginia on Highway 29. Boarding and day boys are accepted in grades 7 to 12, plus one postgraduate year. Girls may enroll as day students. Students are accepted without regard to race, creed or national origin.

The rigorous academic program at Hargrave has ably prepared many generations of students for college entrance. The key to the program is attention to fundamentals. Each student is thoroughly grounded in English, mathematics, science and history. Six computer labs are available.

Hargrave provides a strong and effective program for anyone who wants to succeed. With a student/teacher ratio of 11 to 1, a young man or young woman has the opportunity to achieve and succeed. The Reading and How-To-Study Programs help to rapidly and effectively develop skills essential to academic success. A five-week non-military summer session enables students to take one new subject, two enrichment courses, or two repeat courses.

Many extracurricular activities are offered including swimming, golf, tennis, fishing, skeet, school publications and a variety of interest clubs. Social events are conducted during the year, and 21 interscholastic teams are available for athletic competition. Hargrave has a band for those interested in music. The Boy Scout Troop is the largest in the Blue Ridge Mountain Council.

Hargrave offers the training which develops the characteristics of ethical leadership. Students are shown how to organize, gain the willing cooperation of others, and develop the kind of self-discipline which commands respect and admiration. Hargrave Military Academy is fully accredited by the Virginia Association of Independent Schools as well as the Southern Association of Colleges and Schools, and is a member of the National Association of Independent Schools.

# Discover Harvey...

- *where* classes of 12 to 14 students encourage personal growth as well as academic achievement.

- *where* students find success with teachers who work with students as individuals, both in and out of the classroom, in a warm and supportive environment.

*Harvey is a coeducational college preparatory school enrolling boys and girls of varying abilities in grades 6-12, either as day students or as five-day boarding students.*

## THE HARVEY SCHOOL

260 Jay Street • Katonah, NY 10536 • 914-232-3161
www.harveyschool.org • romanowicz@harveyschool.org

# HEBRON ACADEMY
P.O. Box 309
HEBRON, ME 04238
Tel: 207-966-2100 or Toll-free: 888-432-7664

www.hebronacademy.org

John J. King, *Head of School*

Hebron Academy, founded in 1804, is a boarding and day school located on the eastern edge of the White Mountains in Hebron, Maine. Committed to academic success in preparation for college, Hebron serves girls and boys in grades six through post graduate.

Hebron's traditional college-preparatory curriculum is based on five core courses of English, math, science, history, and foreign language, and is complemented by both Honors and Advanced Placement (AP) offerings. Average class size is 12 students.

There are strong programs in fine and performing arts with courses and extracurricular activities in painting, drawing and sculpture among others, and performance groups in drama, orchestra, and chorus. In addition, the school has a full athletic program and a unique Outdoor Education offering. The Residential Life Program offers many activities and leadership opportunities.

Richly experienced in the teaching, advising, and coaching of young people, the Hebron Academy faculty inspire and guide students to reach their highest potential in mind, body, and spirit.

# THE HILL SCHOOL
## POTTSTOWN, PA

David R. Dougherty, *Headmaster*

At The Hill School, our mission is to prepare young men and women from across the United States and around the world for excellence in school, college, careers, and life. To achieve such scholastic preparation and character development, Hill students learn inside and outside the classrooms: they learn in the dining hall, in the residence halls, in extracurricular activities, in international exchange programs, and on the playing fields. Athletics, in fact, are part of The Hill's curriculum, teaching sportsmanship and self-discipline. Traditions such as twice-weekly chapel services reinforce students' ethical development and nurture their individual spirituality. Naturally, our top priority is providing an outstanding academic environment. The Hill's program is based on the liberal arts and sciences and taught, in small classes, by faculty who reside on campus, serving as dorm parents, coaches, and advisers.

For more information contact:

The Hill School Office of Admission
Pottstown, PA 19464
Toll-free: 888-445-5150 (HILL150)

*Private Schools Illustrated — 1166*

## HILLSDALE ACADEMY

One Academy Lane
Hillsdale, Michigan 49242
517.439.8644
www.hillsdale.edu/academy

*Headmaster: Dr. Kenneth Calvert*

Founded in 1990, the Academy serves as a model kindergarten-through-twelfth grade school. Under the auspices of Hillsdale College, the Academy bases its curriculum on fundamental academic skills, an exploration of the arts and sciences, and an understanding of the foundational tenets of our Judeo-Christian and Greco-Roman heritage. Originally K-8, the Upper School was incorporated in 1998.

Hillsdale Academy offers an academically enriched alternative to students in Hillsdale County and the surrounding area. Students are admitted to the Academy based on the combined strengths of their application and interview, inasmuch as these show evidence of personal motivation.

# The Independent Day School

*Educating Beginners (3-year-olds) through grade eight students*

**Robert L. Fricker, Headmaster**
**115 Laurel Brook Road, Middlefield, CT 06455**

Tel: 860-347-7235   Fax: 860-347-8852   Web: www.idsmiddlefield.org

A co-educational school founded in 1961, The Independent Day School enrolls students with diverse racial, religious and social backgrounds from thirty-two surrounding communities. The student body of 225 experiences a challenging academic curriculum in a supportive enviroment.

The mission of the school is to guide young people toward high standards of scholarship and citizenship, an appreciation of arts, and sound physical, social, and intellectual growth in a nurturing environment. Students are encouraged to display empathy and respect for one another as they become responsible citizens for a changing world.

In the small classes, teachers work with individual students and with cooperative groups to promote each child's academic strengths, problem solving abilities, and critical thinking skills, as well as to stimulate natural curiosity. Science, music, and art classes utilize the natural surroundings of the campus to enrich the curriculum. Every grade presents at least one dramatic production each year. Through the Internet and other academic technologies, students extend their learning. Physical education programs provide recreation and personal physical fitness.

Among our recent graduates, students are attending the following secondary schools: Choate, Loomis Chaffee, Kingswood Oxford, Miss Porter's, Hotchkiss, Hopkins, Northfield Mount Hermon, and The Williams School.

Coeducational Schools — 1167

**Childcare 7:30 A.M.-6:00 P.M.**

*In a rose garden in the heart of the lovely Pacific Heights district*

# HILLWOOD ACADEMIC DAY SCHOOL
**FOR BOYS AND GIRLS IN PRE-KINDERGARTEN THROUGH GRADE 8**

This family school was founded by Mary Libra in 1949. Today Hillwood continues Mrs. Libra's successful school program of quality academics in a productive, happy classroom atmosphere. Hillwood school graduates have an outstanding acceptance record to top quality high schools.

*Good Readers*
**COW HOLLOW KINDERGARTEN**

- Our monthly tuition includes childcare, hot lunch, afternoon snacks and special family rates
- Hillwood is approved by the U.S. State Dept. for foreign students

**PHONE ERIC GRANTZ YEAR-ROUND FOR ENROLLMENT INFORMATION.**

# 931-0400

Hillwood School, 2521 Scott Street, near Broadway, San Francisco, 94115

*Private Schools Illustrated — 1168*

# THE HOTCHKISS SCHOOL
## LAKEVILLE, CT

Robert H. Mattoon, Jr., PhD, *Head of School*

*The aspect of Hotchkiss which gives the school its usefulness and meaning is challenge.* — a student

Hotchkiss is a middle-sized, coeducational boarding school with a demanding academic curriculum and an extensive athletic and extracurricular program. The School strives to help students develop the confidence and clarity of thought necessary to express themselves, make decisions, assume responsibilities, and respond sensitively to the needs of others.

*I came to Hotchkiss in order to receive an excellent academic education. I was successful in obtaining this objective, but I gained a lot more personally—more than I could have imagined three years ago.* — a student

Hotchkiss has long maintained its tradition of academic excellence. Classes range in size from 1 to 16 students. There are 111 full-time faculty members (and administrators) dedicated to the personal growth of each student. Most faculty members live on campus and all take an active role on campus by coaching, advising, leading activities, supervising in dormitories, and participating in the life of the School. Hotchkiss is small enough to retain an intimacy and sense of community which encourage close relationships between faculty members and students. It is also large enough—556 students in grade 9 through 12 & PG—to offer a variety of programs to meet the ever-expanding needs and interests of students.

*The holistic approach to education is what I like about teaching at a boarding school. You're teaching the students, you're coaching the students, you're eating meals with them.* — a faculty member

Extracurricular activities are an important aspect of Hotchkiss life. Students can participate in any of the following clubs and groups: student newspapers, a literary review, radio station, a community service club, choral groups including a gospel choir, instrumental groups, major dramatic productions as well as numerous small-stage performances, scuba diving, computer club, and many other activities. There is ample opportunity to lead. Many senior students serve as proctors in dormitories, head tour guides, discipline committee members, or social committee members. All students participate in a school service program.

*The setting is lovely, the facilities are superb, the students are able, and perhaps more important, the administration is committed to involvement in the daily life of the School.* — a faculty member

Hotchkiss is located on 545 acres of meadows and woodland in the foothills of the Berkshires. The academic facilities and life of the School are centered in the Main Building. Here there are 37 classrooms; 2 computer labs networked for Apple and PC platforms; 7 art studios; a 615-seat auditorium; a black box theater; a dance studio; a language laboratory with video server; and the outstanding Edsel Ford Memorial Library which boasts over 75,000 titles in print, and on video and DVD. Opening in 2005 will be a new music and performing arts wing which will house an auditorium for orchestral performance and new practice rooms. The school chapel and dining hall are attached to either end of the Main Building. The recently renovated Griswold Science Building adjacent to the Main Building boasts 3 floors of laboratory space with independent project rooms, the latest scientific equipment including a scanning electron microscope, a weather station, plant "grow" rooms, a lecture hall equipped for video and computer projection, and state-of-the-art photography studios.

Boarding students at Hotchkiss live in ten dormitories, where they are organized by class year, with about 15 to 25 students per corridor. Faculty members and senior proctors reside on each corridor, providing supervision and guidance. The dormitories are fully networked with voice and data access for every single student; day students enjoy this access as well as boarding students.

*At Hotchkiss, I've learned to push myself and fully discover my capabilities in the classroom and on the field.* — a student

Students participate in sports on many different levels; most interscholastic sports have not only a varsity team, but also a junior varsity and third team. Club sports are intramural. At all levels, students have full use of the school athletic facilities. Hotchkiss has 20 professional tennis courts in addition to a three-court indoor facility, 8 squash courts, 2 hockey rinks, a nine-hole golf course, and an indoor gymnasium complex with a wrestling room, 4 basketball courts, a ten-lane, 25-yard swimming pool, an indoor exercise complex, and a six-lane, all-weather surface track. Hotchkiss' facilities were expanded into a new 200,000-sq. ft. athletic and fitness center, which opened in the fall of 2002. The School borders on Lake Wononscopomuc, the deepest natural lake in Connecticut. Students use the lake for swimming, sailing, ice skating, and scientific research.

Three counselors guide students in the selection of colleges and in the application process. Over 100 college representatives visit the campus each year. The colleges most frequently attended by Hotchkiss students from the last four graduating classes (2000-2003) are: Georgetown, Middlebury, Princeton, University of Virginia, Yale, Brown, Dartmouth, Harvard, Bowdoin, Duke, and Williams.

*Private Schools Illustrated — 1170*

# HOWE MILITARY SCHOOL
HOWE, IN
Tel: 260-562-2131 x221

Since 1884, our objective has been the preparation of young men and women for higher education. Our structured military environment teaches students to take responsibility for themselves. In the JROTC program, Cadets learn to be leaders with integrity and character. Students may apply for grades 5-12, in the college prep curriculum.

It's not easy at Howe; demands are rigorous, but the rewards are great. Graduation requirements are based on the Indiana Honors Diploma standards. Each HS student is required to have a computer, which is networked to teachers on campus. Students must maintain a minimum GPA and conduct rating. Rewards and privileges are based on achievement. Our "whole person" concept includes small structured classes and teachers who care about student success. The 95% level of acceptances at colleges is strong evidence of the success of Howe's program. Howe is an accredited college prep school by the State of Indiana and NCA and a member of ISACS and NAIS.

It's not all work, however. Students have extra-curricular activities such as clubs, organizations, sports teams, recreational trips, and an on-campus canteen for movies and dances, an FM radio station, Ranger group and speech and debate. Affiliated with the Episcopal Church, we accept students of all faiths. Summer Camp is located on nearby Cedar Lake. There are two camps: a six-week, academics camp for HS boys and a recreation/sports camp for boys 9 to 15. Both include sports, waterfront, recreation and ropes.

References are required from 2 teachers and a counselor, and a transcript of grades. Our motto is "Faith and Honor." It's also our way of life. Contact Howe Military School, P.O. Box 240-PS, Howe, IN 46746. Tel: 260-562-2131 x221 or toll-free 888-Go-2-Howe. E-mail: admissions@howemilitary.com. Home page: www.howemilitary.com.

# HOWE SUMMER CAMP
## HOWE, IN
Tel: 260-562-2131 x221

Dr. Duane Van Orden, *Superintendent*

The Howe Military School Summer Camp is ideally located among 45 acres of woodland on the shores of Cedar Lake and enjoys excellent facilities.

There are two basic camps:

1) a six-week, credit academics camp with recreational activities for boys in the 9th and 10th grades
2) a recreation and sports camp for boys 9 to 15 years old

Both camps include military and recreational activities featuring baseball, soccer, basketball, tennis, golf, canoe trips, swimming, sailing, nature study, handicrafts, archery, air riflery, and a ropes course.

The camp is broken into two sessions of three weeks each or one six-week session. High School boys must attend for six weeks.

Howe's Summer Camp is accredited by the American Camping Association and has been since the inception of the ACA. Howe Summer Camp is one of the few in the USA which can make that claim.

The six-week session in 2005 runs from June 19 through July 29. The first three-week session is from June 19 through July 8 and the second three-week session is from July 10 through July 29.

Tuition, uniforms, spending money and crafts: $3300 for six weeks ($1900 for a three-week session).

Contact Howe Military School, Admission Office, P.O. Box 240-PS, Howe, IN 46746. Tel: 260-562-2131 x230 or toll-free 888-Go-2-Howe. E-mail: admissions@howemilitary.com. Home page: www.howemilitary.com.

*Private Schools Illustrated — 1172*

# HOBGOOD ACADEMY
Committed to excellence—academically, physically, and socially.

Home to a dedicated faculty, varsity girls and boys sports, and a wide variety of clubs and organizations, Hobgood Academy has all the sophistication of a large school with the simplicity of a small-town environment.

- Faculty: 100% of high school faculty sponsor extra-curricular activities; over 85% of full-time faculty have teaching certification or advanced degrees
- Athletics: Baseball and Softball, Basketball, Cheerleading, Golf, Football, Ladies Soccer, and Volleyball
- Clubs and Organizations: Battle of the Books, Beta Club, Drama, FCA, Journalism, Yearbook, Service Organizations, and many others
- Honors and Awards: Harvard Club recognition for Outstanding Student and Faculty; District Math Competition Winner; Former District Quiz Bowl Winner; Former Winner of the prestigious Wachovia Cup for outstanding school-wide athletics

Find out what Hobgood Academy has to offer you today!!
www.hobgoodacademy.com

# THE HUDSON SCHOOL

601 Park Ave.
HOBOKEN, NJ 07030
Tel: 201-659-8335
Fax: 201-222-3669

Suellen F. Newman, BA, MA, *Director*
Gene L. Noce, BA, MA, *College Guidance Counselor*
Jack Coggins, BA, *Dean of Students*

Founded in 1978, The Hudson School conducts a diversified and rigorous academic program for children in grades five through twelve. Students come from Hoboken and more than forty neighboring communities in Hudson, Bergen, Union, Middlesex, Morris and Essex counties, as well as from New York City and overseas.

The curriculum, designed for bright, achievement-oriented children, includes English, history, science, math, computer science, philosophy, French, Spanish, German, Japanese, Greek and Latin. The school also offers many elective courses in the fine and performing arts as well as co-curricular theatre activities. Hudson's emphasis on each child's creativity is reflected in such extracurricular activities as literary publications, choral singing, instrumental music instruction, yoga, video production, calligraphy, and dancing. Foreign study opportunities and sports are included in the program. Currently, there are eleven athletic teams. All students are required to perform 20 hours per year of community service, beginning in grade eight.

The Hudson School offers a full high school academic program, including twelve AP courses. Hudson graduates attend the finest colleges in the United States and abroad. There is an international and ethnically diverse student body, and a need-blind admissions policy. The Hudson School actively encourages high school students to spend a year studying abroad and sponsors trips to other countries during the year and in the summer.

# THE HUN SCHOOL OF PRINCETON
176 Edgerstoune Rd.
PRINCETON, NJ 08540

James M. Byer '62, BA, MA, EdS, EdD, *Headmaster*

Message from Dr. James Byer:

Experiencing tradition, educating for today, and preparing for the future requires a delicate balance and a commitment to purposeful change. The Hun School is at such a stage in its history. Students at The Hun School are expected to make sound moral judgments while they participate in a rigorous scholastic program designed to excite curiosity and stimulate critical thinking and analysis. Competent, caring faculty work closely with students to promote excellence and self-esteem in an environment with high but fair expectations. Students are encouraged to be active learners, ask questions, write across the curriculum, and defend their thinking. The curriculum reflects the School's commitment to traditional college coursework with emphasis on the relevancy of one's studies. Additionally, elective courses and programs are available to supplement students' academic backgrounds and experiences.

The Hun School is a School with a conscience. Kindness, respect, and trust are part of everyday life. Community service is expected here, for we know that our future leaders must give of themselves to others in the interest of a better society.

As both an alumnus and the current Headmaster, I well understand the inspiration The Hun School provides to encourage its students to be open-minded, observant, disciplined, and challenged. Today, it is essential for students to respond to an increasingly diverse world. The Hun School's goal is to graduate articulate, confident, sensitive students who are well-prepared for world citizenship.

Founded in 1914 by Dr. John Gale Hun, our fully accredited, coeducational, internationally populated School serves approximately 570 students in grades 6-PG. Three dormitories house 150 resident students in grades 9-PG.

In order to be responsive to the needs and goals of each student, the comprehensive curriculum at The Hun School is complemented by three computer centers, a 50,000 volume, on-line library/information center, a Writing and Peer Tutoring Center, a Study Strategies Program, a highly regarded athletic program, and an array of notable extracurricular activities. Advanced placement work is available in all course areas, and selected students may apply for advanced classes at Princeton University and other nearby colleges. The Hun School's Academic Learning Skills Program, limited to thirty students, provides individual, specialized instruction for capable and motivated students with specific learning disabilities. The International Student Program, one of the oldest established programs in the country, is designed to help students master the English language through English as a Second Language courses, to orient them to American culture, and to continue course work in all academic areas, enabling them to qualify for admission to enumerable American colleges and universities.

Students take advantage of cultural and educational opportunities in the town of Princeton, most notably at McCarter Theater and the McCormick Museum of Art, as well as in New York and Philadelphia. Interscholastic and intramural athletic opportunities abound and are an important part of the curriculum. The School has five athletic fields, a gymnasium, an outdoor track, and eight tennis courts. Activities include numerous student publications, band, chorus, cheerleading, Honor Council, Key Club, Student Government, and the Cum Laude Society. There are chess, outdoor education, creative writing, drama, Asian, French, and Spanish clubs.

The Student Activities Center, housing photography, music, woodworking, and arts studios, as well as a television studio, was completed in 1975. In 1986, the School doubled the size of its Academic Center. Recently, the library and computer based information resources, as well as facilities for mathematics, science, and computer science, were expanded, the Dining Hall was renovated, extensive new landscaping and campus recreation spaces were added, the Heart of Hun project completed, and construction of the new Athletic Center was started.

Our comprehensive summer program includes a five-week boarding and day summer school, two programs for international students, a summer theater program, and a five-week Hun Camp for boys and girls ages 6-12.

Educationally committed families are invited to explore our programs and to consider a partnership with The Hun School. We welcome campus visits during the school day. For more information, please contact the Admissions Office by telephone at (609) 921-7600, Ext. 2380, by fax at (609) 279-9398, or by e-mail at admiss@hunschool.org. You can also visit our web site, www.hunschool.org.

*Private Schools Illustrated — 1176*

# HYDE SCHOOLS
www.hyde.edu

Malcolm W. Gauld, *President*

| BATH, ME | WOODSTOCK, CT |
|---|---|
| Laurie G. Hurd, *Head of School* | Duncan McCrann, *Head of School* |

Hyde School is a coeducational, college preparatory school for boarding and day students in grades 9-12. Joseph W. Gauld founded Hyde School in 1966 in Bath, ME in response to a system of education he believed had become overly preoccupied with students' talents and insufficiently focused on their character. A second campus opened in 1996 in Connecticut in response to a growing demand for Hyde's character-based education. Hyde Schools value attitude more than aptitude, effort more than ability, and character more than talent and embody the belief that character is primarily taught by example. This means that teachers and parents need an ongoing program to address their own character and self-discovery.

The Hyde curriculum is built on the belief that each individual has the potential to achieve personal excellence. Hyde Schools strive to locate, encourage and develop this potential in families. Throughout its curriculum, which includes for all students, academics, athletics, performing arts, community service, and wilderness experiences, Hyde upholds the core value of Five Words—Courage, Integrity, Leadership, Curiosity, and Concern. Hyde's program has evolved over 35 years to effectively focus on three emphases:

- A fully integrated program of character development—character is not an adjunct of the program. It is the foundation from which all other curriculum is developed.
- Family renewal, resulting from true parent participation—parents are not involved to merely support the work of the faculty; they work to develop their own character. Hyde's Family Education Program is its hallmark.
- College preparation—98% of Hyde graduates are accepted to four-year colleges. Hyde graduates have enrolled at Babson, Bowdoin, Bucknell, Carleton, Carnegie-Mellon, Clark, Colgate, Columbia, Cornell, Dickinson, Duke, Eckerd, Georgetown, Hamilton, Hobart, Kenyon, Lewis & Clark, Lynchburg College, Middlebury, Northwestern, Roanoke, Rensselaer Polytechnic Institute, Rutgers, Skidmore, Wheaton, and the Universities of British Columbia, Colorado, Michigan, Oregon, Southern California, Texas, Univ. of Hartford, Univ. of Redlands, Univ. of Vermont, Vanderbilt, and Univ. of Virginia.

Although some schools may match or exceed Hyde's performance with one or two of these emphases, Hyde submits that it is the best, and indeed the only choice for prospective families who seek to accept the challenge of all three. The Bath, ME campus is located on the majestic, historic former estate of shipbuilder John S. Hyde. The coastal city of Bath is a 45-minute drive from Portland Jetport and a 2½-hour drive north of Boston.

The Woodstock, CT campus is located in the northeastern corner of the state on the grounds of a former Catholic women's college. The campus is a 30-minute drive from Providence, a 1½-hour commute to Boston or Hartford, and 25 miles from the Sturbridge Village exit of the Massachusetts Turnpike.

For additional information contact:

Hyde School Admissions Office
616 High Street
Bath, ME 04530-5002
Tel: 207-443-7101
Fax: 207-442-9346
E-mail: bath.admissions@hyde.edu

Hyde School Admissions Office
P.O. Box 237
Woodstock, CT 06281-0237
Tel: 860-963-4736
Fax: 860-928-0612
E-mail: woodstock.admissions@hyde.edu

Website: www.hyde.edu

*Private Schools Illustrated — 1178*

# KENT SCHOOL
### KENT, CT
Tel: 860-927-6111

The Rev. Richardson W. Schell, *Headmaster*

Kent is a co-educational, college preparatory, boarding school in northwestern Connecticut for students in grades 9 through 12. The school has 550 students from 32 states and 22 countries. Kent was established in 1906 by Fr. Frederick H. Sill, an Episcopal priest whose vision of education was based on simplicity of life, directness of purpose and self-reliance. Originally a boys school, Kent became co-educational in 1960 when it established a co-ordinate division for girls on a separate campus. After 30 years as a 2 campus school, Kent has consolidated its operations onto one campus. Construction of the new facilities was completed in September of 1992.

From its founding Kent has been a place for young people to grow, to learn and to live in a dynamic community. The school is dedicated to enabling students to develop their intellectual gifts in order to increase their knowledge of themselves and their relationships with one another and the world. In reflection of its Episcopal heritage, the school also seeks to develop in students an ethical foundation of living based on religious teachings and practice.

The academic program and school life are structured to create an environment in which boys and girls can become self-reliant, disciplined, caring, young adults, ready and able to succeed in their college-level studies and to lead productive lives in a rapidly changing world. The Kent experience is enriched by the shared school life of students and faculty families representing a broad spectrum of cultural, economic and geographic backgrounds.

The academic program emphasizes the liberal arts in a curriculum of traditional rigor. Advanced Placement courses are offered in every discipline, including computer programming, economics, art history and environmental science. The extra-curricular program provides opportunities in sports for every student. In addition there are programs in vocal and instrumental music (ensembles as well as private lessons), drama, art and dance. Through faculty sponsored activities students may pursue art, creative writing, independent study or volunteer social work. There are also student led clubs and activities.

The Kent faculty (16 years average teaching experience) reflects a fine balance of experience, advanced study, and youthful enthusiasm. A number are successful writers and lecturers in their various academic fields. Most have experienced the advantages of travel and graduate study. The student-faculty ratio is 7 to 1. Most faculty members live in school housing or in apartments in student dormitories. Nine members of the faculty are graduates of Kent, including the Headmaster. New students are admitted at all levels, but the majority enter for the full four years. Kent seeks students who possess the motivation and determination to invest themselves to the best of their abilities in the full life of the school.

# KENTS HILL SCHOOL
## KENTS HILL, ME

Founded in 1824, Kents Hill School is a small, coeducational, college preparatory school located 10 minutes from Maine's capital city, Augusta. Set on a hill overlooking the Belgrade Lakes region, the School includes 500 acres of private land, including a state-of-the-art on-campus ski and snowboard facility.

Kents Hill's hallmarks are these:

1. **Small classes**—The average size is 10, and several are considerably smaller, permitting a great deal of individual attention.
2. **A committed, residential faculty**—Several of our teachers have been at Kents Hill for more than twenty years. Virtually all faculty members live on campus, making them readily available for help outside the classroom.
3. **The Alfond Athletics Center**—The $7 million facility includes an ice arena, a gymnasium, a fitness center, and locker rooms completed in September 2000.
4. **A top-notch program in competitive skiing and snowboarding**—The program is supported by the school's lighted ski slope with snowmaking and a small snowboard park. 8 kilometers of cross-country trails wind through the campus' forest. The new Liz Cross Mellen lodge at the top of the facility provides students with tuning and storage rooms, and a place to warm up in between runs!
5. **The Learning Skills Center**—A specially-staffed program which provides tutorial support for students with weak organizational and study skills or moderate learning disabilities.
6. **Extraordinary art facilities**—The George Bass Art Center provides our art students with exceptional facilities and instruction. Nine potters' wheels, a woodworking center, a sculpting studio, a painting studio, a darkroom, and individual studio space for students preparing college portfolios are a few of the center's features.

7. **Outing Club opportunities**—The Outdoor Skills Program offers students interested in the out-of-doors regular opportunities to go hiking, canoeing, and camping in many beautiful locations in Maine's wilderness areas.
8. **An abiding concern for ethical issues**—Honesty, altruism, compassion, and courage are among the characteristics the school encourages and seeks to address in its daily dialogue with its students. All students participate in the school's Community Service Program, where teachers and students spend time in the community volunteering at local nursing homes, homeless shelters, churches, schools, and businesses.
9. **A strong concern for environmental issues**—Science at Kents Hill is exciting and relevant to today's environmental issues. Kents Hill utilizes its setting on several acres of fields, streams and forest surrounded by two lakes and several farms, to conduct extensive fieldwork in the out-of-doors. Environmental issues are explored outside of the Science classroom and are woven into other subject areas, including art, history, and English.

These are just a few of Kents Hill School's highlights. Kents Hill is looking for young men and women of sound character who are interested in a thorough academic preparation for college in a warm and supportive school environment. We hope you will come for a visit to meet current Kents Hill students and faculty, and to see our unique school for yourself.

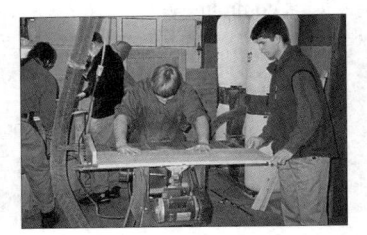

*Private Schools Illustrated — 1182*

# KING & LOW-HEYWOOD THOMAS SCHOOL
1450 Newfield Ave.
STAMFORD, CT 06905
Tel: 203-322-3496 Fax: 203-461-9988
Web: www.klht.org

At KLHT, we live our mission as a diverse, vibrant learning community dedicated to helping each student reach his or her fullest potential. Beyond racial, ethnic and socioeconomic variety, we also recognize and value differences in learning styles. We are proud of our ability to provide the challenges, the nurturing and the support that each student needs to develop as a thinker, an artist, an athlete, a leader, and a citizen of the global community.

The Lower School at KLHT encompasses pre-kindergarten (age 4) through fifth grade. Our developmental program addresses the mental, social, physical and emotional interactions that a child experiences each day. In first grade, the basic program of reading, writing, spelling, math, social studies and science is augmented by foreign language, art, drama, computer science, library and physical education. By fifth grade, we expect intellectual growth to be complemented by more independent study, as students work on long-term research projects. Our life-skills curriculum includes values, manners, mutual respect and social skills.

KLHT's Middle School, sixth through eighth grades, provides a challenging academic program balanced by full participation in arts, athletics, and community service. Academic subjects include English, geography, history, mathematics, science, modern languages, ethics, studio art and performing arts. Every Middle School student participates in an annual drama or musical production as well as a full year of athletics. Based on the idea that they learn best when pursuing personal interests, we offer students many opportunities to explore what excites them. We encourage students to seek out and share information, to set high standards for themselves, and to accept ever-increasing responsibilities. The underlying points of focus are priority skills—communication, writing, speaking, viewing (reading and media), artistic and creative expression, physical ability—and character development. Team teaching by grade, along with an effective advisory system, assures that each child receives thoughtful individual attention.

The Upper School, ninth through twelfth grades, provides a broad program of traditional courses along with Advanced Placement and honors classes and support courses for students with diagnosed learning differences. Specialized courses such as British literature, micro- and macroeconomics and genetics are offered for qualified students. Graduation requirements also include participation in musical or dramatic productions as well as sports. Extracurricular opportunities address a variety of interests, from student publications to Model UN to community service. No matter what the venue, students learn to take risks, express themselves in new and different ways, and work together toward common goals. College counseling also is a focus throughout the Upper School years, with grade-specific goals to ensure that each student is well-prepared for the college application process by senior year.

# THE JOHN COOPER SCHOOL
THE WOODLANDS, TX
Tel: 281-367-0900   Fax: 281-298-5715
Web: www.johncooper.org
Michael F. Maher, *Head of School*

The John Cooper School is a K-12 non-sectarian, co-educational, college preparatory day school, located on a wooded 43-acre campus in The Woodlands, Texas. The mission of The John Cooper School is to provide a challenging education in a caring environment to a diverse group of select students enabling them to become creative thinkers, responsible citizens and leaders, and lifetime learners. The school focuses on the development of each child—intellectually, artistically and athletically—within the context of a strong academic program taught by a nationally recognized faculty. Organized community service programs are offered at all levels of the school.

Since 1988, The John Cooper School has grown from 175 students to a current K-12 enrollment of 880. Current facilities include: a lower school building (K-5) with adjacent playgrounds, covered basketball pavilion and outdoor learning centers—the Children's Garden, Arboretum and Environmental Science Center; and a middle/upper school for grades 6-8 and 9-12. All Cooper students utilize two fully equipped gymnasiums, softball and soccer fields, a cross country course and track and field facility, tennis courts, baseball field; and extensive visual arts facilities nicknamed "the art barn."

From K-12, The John Cooper School curriculum is traditional and conforms to standards recommended by the National Association of Independent Schools (NAIS). Admission is competitive and students are selected largely on the basis of aptitude and potential for success in a rigorous college preparatory program of study. Class size is limited to ensure individualized attention and to facilitate open and regular communication with teachers. The Class of 2005 has 81 members, of whom three have been named National Merit Finalists, 10 as Commended Scholars, three as scholars in the National Hispanic Recognition Program, and one a Presidential Scholar Semifinalist.

Student athletes compete on 14 different athletic teams. Varsity athletes compete in the Southwest Preparatory Conference.

The John Cooper School is accredited by the Independent Schools Association of the Southwest and is a member of NAIS, the College Entrance Examination Board, Educational Records Bureau, National Association of College Admission Counselors and the Cum Laude Society. Confidential, need-based financial aid is available. Cooper welcomes students of any race, color, religion or national/ethnic background, and does not discriminate on the basis of physical handicap or gender.

# KIMBALL UNION
## A C A D E M Y
### Meriden, New Hampshire

Michael J. Schafer, BA, Colby College, MEd, Harvard Univ, *Head of School*

Founded in 1813, Kimball Union Academy is the 15th oldest boarding school in the country. Kimball Union's unique location in the Upper Connecticut River Valley and its proximity to Dartmouth College have long made it the preferred choice for both boarding and day students seeking an educational experience to develop the whole person as scholar, athlete, artist and global citizen.

The strong four-year course of study prepares students for programs in major colleges and universities. Over 100 courses are offered including 15 advanced placement courses across all disciplines. The average class size is 11 students with a student-faculty ratio of 6:1. Our unique environmental studies program includes a cross curricular approach, an AP offering and a greenhouse, and a 750-acre tract of land on nearby Snow Mountain that provides an outdoor "classroom." Performing and visual arts are offered both within the curriculum and as extra-curricular activities in the spectacular Flickinger Arts Center. Sports offered include hockey, football, lacrosse, Nordic and alpine skiing, field hockey, basketball, softball, baseball soccer, mountain biking, equestrian, rugby, tennis and cross country. Kimball Union competes in the Lakes Region League, among others.

The main campus covers over 800 acres of rolling hillside in the picturesque village of Meriden just 13 miles from Dartmouth College and its resources. Facilities include a magnificent dining hall, a beautiful arts center, a science building with a new environmental studies wing, a state-of-the art hockey arena with seasonal turf, athletic center, new fitness center, library, computer, language and science labs, student center and indoor pool. There are 9 dormitories housing from 5 to 50 students.

Kimball Union's highly qualified and dedicated faculty is committed to serving our students and families. Our strong advisor system provides students with support for their academic and social needs. Recent initiatives include expanded student life services, a peer mentorship program and more student leadership opportunities.

The Academy is committed to fulfilling its mission to "discover with each student the right path to academic mastery, to creativity and to responsibility." Members of our community are guided by our Honor Code, which reflects our core value and promotes honesty, compassion and mutual respect.

*Private Schools Illustrated — 1186*

# THE LAMPLIGHTER SCHOOL

11611 Inwood Rd.
DALLAS, TX 75229

Tel: 214-369-9201   Fax: 214-369-5540
www.thelamplighterschool.org

The Lamplighter School is an independent, co-educational day school for students in pre-kindergarten (ages three and four) through fourth grade. Founded in 1953, Lamplighter School's motto remains, "A student is not a vessel to be filled, but a lamp to be lighted." Lamplighter holds membership in the National Association of Independent Schools and is accredited by the Independent Schools Association of the Southwest. Lamplighter was designated an EnergyStar awardee by the EPA in 2003. It is also a Blue Ribbon School of Excellence.

The purpose of the school is to bring each child to the highest level of potential. Lamplighter's teachers believe that children are naturally curious, creative, and eager. They encourage learning by doing, promote cooperation rather than competition, and have high expectations for the pursuit of academic excellence. These objectives are best realized in a setting